Yeshe Tsogel

The Beloved of Love

I am the beloved of love,
The queen of great bliss,
The *dakini* of perfect love.
In the triumph of love,
Where no wound may
Find an opening,
No weapon may pierce,
For love is the supreme,
Shield and sanctuary,
For love casts no shadow.
Nor may be denied.

To the Love that remains when the lover and beloved vanish.

Sacred Love
Buddhist Tantric Poems

Sophia Dalle Rubenstein

*To Namgay Dawa Rinpoche,
Iho Ontul Rinpoche,
Khenpo Tsewong,
Khenpo Karthur Rinpoche
and Namkhai Norbu.*

*To all Buddhists in all lineages
for the sake of all sentient beings.*

*For my truest love,
my beloved amongst all men.*

Tsalki –Anna Lieb-Dubino and B. Love

Table of Contents

Acknowledgements	xi
Foreword	xii
Preface	xv
Introduction	xvi
The Garland	21
To Ask For Nothing	22
For All Else	23
The Splendour of Love	24
Nying-je	26
If I Do Not Have Love	27
Citadel of the Heart	28
There Is Only Love	30
Dakinis and Daka	33
How Do I Love Thee?	34
Ever So Graceful	35
Seal of Mahamudra	36
The Kiss of the Vajra	38
Mortal Samsara	39
The Golden Lotus	41
Sacred Kiss	42
The Kiss of Everlasting Love	43
Your Kiss of Liberation	44
Where There Is Love	46
Immortal Caress	47
The Divine Kiss	49
Night of Love	50
The Crown Tantric Embrace	53
Of Sorrows and Joys Taken	54

The Mala of Love	55
In the Splendour of Love	56
You Will Drink My Tears	58
The Kiss of Liberation	59
My Beloved Love	61
By Love Alone	62
For As Long as I Shall Live	63
Oh, My Beloved	64
In the Embrace of Bodhicitta	66
Samarasya	68
Consort	71
With No Regrets	72
The Respite of Rigpa	74
Bodhicitta Rises	76
For M	78
I Wait	80
The Nostalgia of Nirvana	82
True Loves First Kiss	83
The Crown of the Dharmakaya	85
Your Mala of Love	86
Buddhist Tonglen	87
Crown of Skulls	89
Death and Impermanence	90
Effulgent in the Grace	91
Bodhicitta	92
The Cloudless Sky	94
The Kiss of the Dakinis	95
The Kiss of the Dakinis	95

Surrender to Love	97
In the Essence of Tonglen	98
Chod	100
Accoutrements	102
The Heart of Forgiveness	103
Blessed Garment of Love	105
The Kiss of the Dharmakaya	106
Never for My Sake Alone	109
Utterly Beyond	110
Blessings	111
The End of Samsara	112
Sacred Kiss of Liberation	115
The Mala of Radiant Love	116
A Garland of Bodhicitta	117
A Single Lamp Is Lit	119
Mirror, Lucid	120
No End to Bodhicitta	122
Far Better	123
Mamo Ekajati	125
Mantra of Liberation	126
The Secret Language	128
Only Love	129
In the Merciful Cathedral	131
For the Sake of All Beings	132
Only Love Is Not Written on Water	135
O Let Me Be the Salvation	136
Vajra Chain	138
The Garland of Empty Space	140

Cherish Love	141
Abiding	143
The One Taste	144
Oh Beloved	147
The Lamp to Guide the Way	148
The Purpose of Love	150
Until My Last Breath	151
On the Altar of Love	152
Of Rigpa	154
Oh Great Primordial Liberation!	155
What Is Love?	157
Crown of Endless Luminosity	158
Surrender	159
'Though Its Very Essence	161
No One's Blood	162
Unfathomable Love	164
The Garland of Bodhicitta	166
This Crown of Love	168
O Belovèd	169
The Ecstasy of Love	171
In the Stillness Deep	172
Beloved Consort	174
For the Love of Rigpa	177
How May I Liken My Love for Thee	178
Kadak	180
Artists	184
For the Liberation of All Beings,	186

Rinpoche Namgay Dawa

To Rinpoche Namgay Dawa
for his encouragement, elegant support
and compassionate teachings
that have given me the courage
to create this work for the public.

To Ngak'chang Rinpoche for his kindness
and teachings and always giving me face.

To Lama Michael Gregory for his kindness.

To my brother Stephen Cornine
for all of his hard work editing,
organizing and support.

Foreword

Sophia Dalle, drawing deeply from the well of her own life experiences, transforms these moments into poetic verses that resonate with wisdom. Each poem reflects her journey, shaped by the profound teachings of Buddhism, offering readers a glimpse into the peaceful acceptance of life's impermanence.

This collection is not merely a reflection of her thoughts but a harmonious symphony of her spiritual insights, blending the serenity of Buddhist philosophy with the rawness of human emotion.

Through these poems, she invites us to witness the transformative power of mindfulness, compassion, and understanding – elements that have enriched her path and now is revealed to us.

I wish her continued success in all her artistic endeavors.

Dungsay Namgay Dawa Rinpoche

༄༅། །བྱང་མའི་རྡོ་རྗེ་འཛིན་མཁར་གསར་ཡེ་ཤེས་སྙིང་པོ་ཆོས་ཚོགས། །

THE VAJRA SEAT OF KYABJE DUDJOM JIGDRAL YESHE DORJE IN NORTH AMERICA

Under the Spiritual Direction of H.H. Dungsey Namgay Dawa Rimpoche

---

Sophia Dalle, drawing deeply from the well of her own life experiences, transforms these moments into poetic verses that resonate with wisdom. Each poem reflects her journey, shaped by the profound teachings of Buddhism, offering readers a glimpse into the peaceful acceptance of life's impermanence.

This collection is not merely a reflection of her thoughts but a harmonious symphony of her spiritual insights, blending the serenity of Buddhist philosophy with the rawness of human emotion.

Through these poems, she invites us to witness the transformative power of mindfulness, compassion, and understanding—elements that have enriched her path and now is revealed to us.

I wish her continued success in all her artistic endeavors.

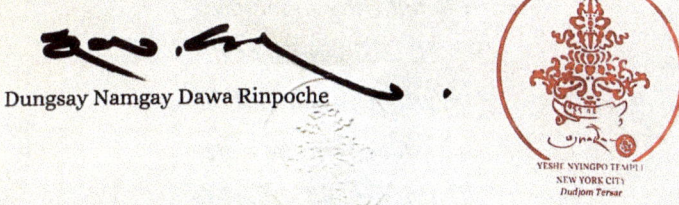

Dungsay Namgay Dawa Rinpoche

Yeshe Nyingpo Temple
📍 19 West 16th Street, New York, NY 10011
📞 212-691-8523

Orgyen Cho Dzong Retreat
📍 5345 Route 81, Greenville, NY 12083

Contact Us
✉ thefearlesswisdom@gmail.com
🌐 dudjomtersar.org

Oh Rest! the weary mind!
Do not cling to phenomena.
Do not cling to appearances.
Do not cling to thoughts.
Do not cling to sorrows.
All will vanish as if
Written on water. Oh!
Rest, rest, in the state
That is beyond suffering.
Rest in the embrace
Of Bodhicitta for the sake
Of all sentient beings.

Preface

These poems arise not only from silence but from the light that opens within suffering, and from the long path of healing and return. Each waking moment becomes the possibility of a poem or prose when lived in sacred awareness. I offer my work as a possible expression of such gratitude for the teachers, visible and unseen, who have shown the way through darkness and into clarity, and to the light, to comfort those who perchance when reading my work at that juxtaposition of a moment's reflection something opens indescribable in words, and to those who love.

All proceeds from this publication are dedicated to the support and well-being of elderly Buddhist nuns, whose devotion and humility often remain unseen, though their merit sustains the world.

May these words bring benefit to all who read them. May they offer rest to the weary, light to the lost, and a gentle reminder that nothing, once touched by love, is ever truly broken.

Sacred Love is a journey beyond form and concept, a sacred transmission birthed from visionary states of exalted love—where the open heart awakens to the eternal dance of union.

Through luminous verse and piercing prose, Sophia reveals the sacred threshold where the human and divine entwine, where lovers and solitary seekers alike dissolve boundaries and awaken to the ineffable truth of non-dual union.

This collection is a rare offering of the living Dharma—a doorway into the depths of spiritual love as ultimate liberation, a bridge between the vast heart of Vajrayana and Dzogchen, and the awakening pulse of Western mysticism.

In the radiant silence of Bodhicitta,
love unfolds
as the primal ground of all being—
a living light
that merges emptiness and bliss
into one luminous whole—
the great seal of Mahamudra.

Sacred Love

The Garland

Upon the garland of liberated lifetimes,
I stamped the never-ending image of
My beloved's face, whose mirror, lucid,
Revealed every moment's love in grace,
And in the clarity of exulted, empty space,
Where wisdom's awareness knows no veil,
My love for you is as the dawning of the
Supreme *Dharmakaya* itself, the great
Unborn uncreated expanse of love eternal,
Wherein even death holds no sway.

To Ask For Nothing

The radiant heart
Needs no adornment
To live in love, to ask
For nothing, to be,
The very love you seek,
Hence
The golden bough
Of loves succor and
Grace will not fail thee,
Not now,
Not ever.

For All Else

For if you have not love
In your heart for all,
You have nothing,
For all else is
Written upon water.

The Splendour of Love

Residing in the Citadel of the Dharmakaya,
Where the splendour of love is endless,
The Light of the divine never grows dim.
The three impure doors of cyclic existence
Here are no more, only Bodhicitta.
Rays of luminosity radiate and the
Appearances of obscurations are dissolved
Unwavering is the ultimate truth of
Compassion in all its Holy effusion
I bow down.

Nying-je

Lord of the heart,
Oh, beloved, what is
The noble heart?
It is the clear aspect of mind,
When, in harmony
With the subtle body,
In recognition of
Its underlying nature,
Which is the
Essence of love,
Its undying, never-born,
Never separate from
The beyond eternal
Essence of love,
The crown of which
Never falters.
Speak to me only of love.

If I Do Not Have Love

If I do not have love,
If I have only knowledge,
Conceptual, impersonal,
If I have not the language
Of the heart,
The truest love,
The love that is in all its
Ineffable glory, the *Dharmakaya*.
If I do not love,
I have sadly mistaken the truth.

Citadel of the Heart

In the citadel of the heart,
Where the truth is found,
Not a mouthful of lies.
In the citadel of the heart,
Where all are equal,
The portal to the divine has
Always been open.
It never closes.
By love alone, it is by love,
Pure, pristine perception,
Dharmakaya,
Nirmanakay,
Sambogakaya all.
The great seal of *Mahamudra,*
All by love alone.

–Mark Kusek

There Is Only Love

Before the body,
there was love.
Before the breath,
there was love.
Before the "I,"
there was love.
Before birth,
and after death—
there is only love.

Only love may embrace
what cannot be held,
for it is the very essence—
even in silence,
it dwells.

Love does not need
to be earned,
nor will it disappear
with time.

Love can never truly be lost,
for love never forgets.
Love will always remember.

It needs no altar,
no god.

Before your wounds,
and after all your pain,
when all else vanishes—
love will remain.

Love will remain,
as it has never
not existed.

For the only truth is love—
even in the ashes,
and the dust
of your bones.

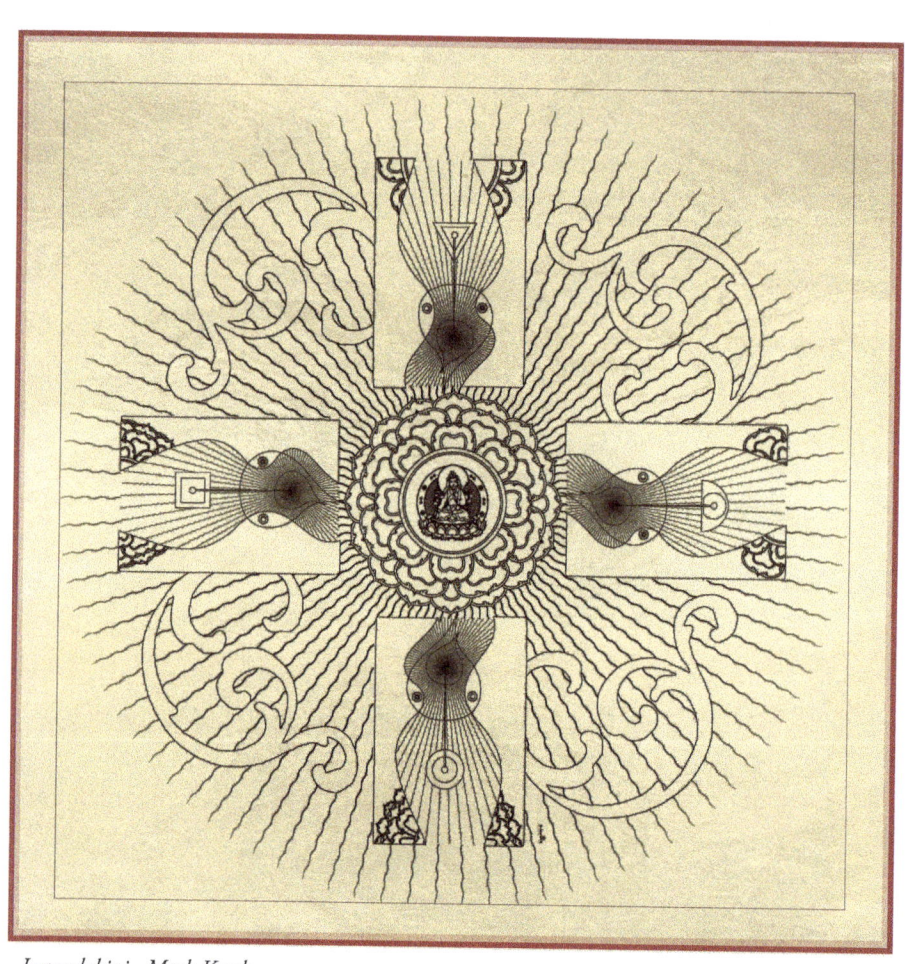

Jnanadakini –Mark Kusek

Dakinis and Daka

Sisters and brothers, Dakas.
Om A'aḥ Hung Bendzra Guru Jnana Sagara Bam
Ha Ri Ni Sa Siddhi Hungḥ
Come and play amongst the light effervescent,
Where dawn and night are the same,
Where the radiant heart of love
Never ends,
Where the Buddhas drink
The holy waters of love,
Where there is no
Thought of mine or thine,
Where thine eye is
Single and full of light.
Come and dance with me,
Naked in supernal bliss
As a secret, now revealed.
Come and dance with me!
Om hrih bam jana dakini mandarava ayu siddhi ja hung.

How Do I Love Thee?

How do I love thee?
Oh, how do I love thee?
Do I love thee for my sake alone?
Nay, I love thee, my beloved,
For the sake of all sentient beings,
For thy sake in samsara,
In liberation, in the radiant heart
Of effulgent, never-ending divine grace.
How will I care for thee?
I will care for thee, and cherish thee
Above my own self, in the endless realm
Of love, so beyond eternal concepts,
Untouchable by mortality.
In the apocryphal writings
I have loved thee,
In the mantras of Buddhism
I have loved thee.
I have loved thee through the vedas.
In the greatest of darkness, I have loved thee.
There has been no time I have not loved thee,
For love loves itself through all things,
For love knows only love and naught else.
By love alone will I always love thee.

Ever So Graceful

Ever so graceful
Is the love
That endures,
Reborn through
Incarnations,
Where transitory
Clouds may vanish.
The thorns of *samsar*
Disappear in
The heartbeat of this love.
Ever so graceful
Is your love
In all of its tender mercy,
The destiny of which
Survives the grave.

Seal of Mahamudra

'Though its very essence
Is unborn,
It gives life to all.
Beyond eternal,
It cannot be annihilated.
It is, oh, my beloved,
The very love we all
Have sought over and over,
Through far too many cycles
Of sorrows;
Yet, it has never left us.
This love is
The seal of *Mahamudra*.
Let us realize the
One taste in
Co-emergent bliss.

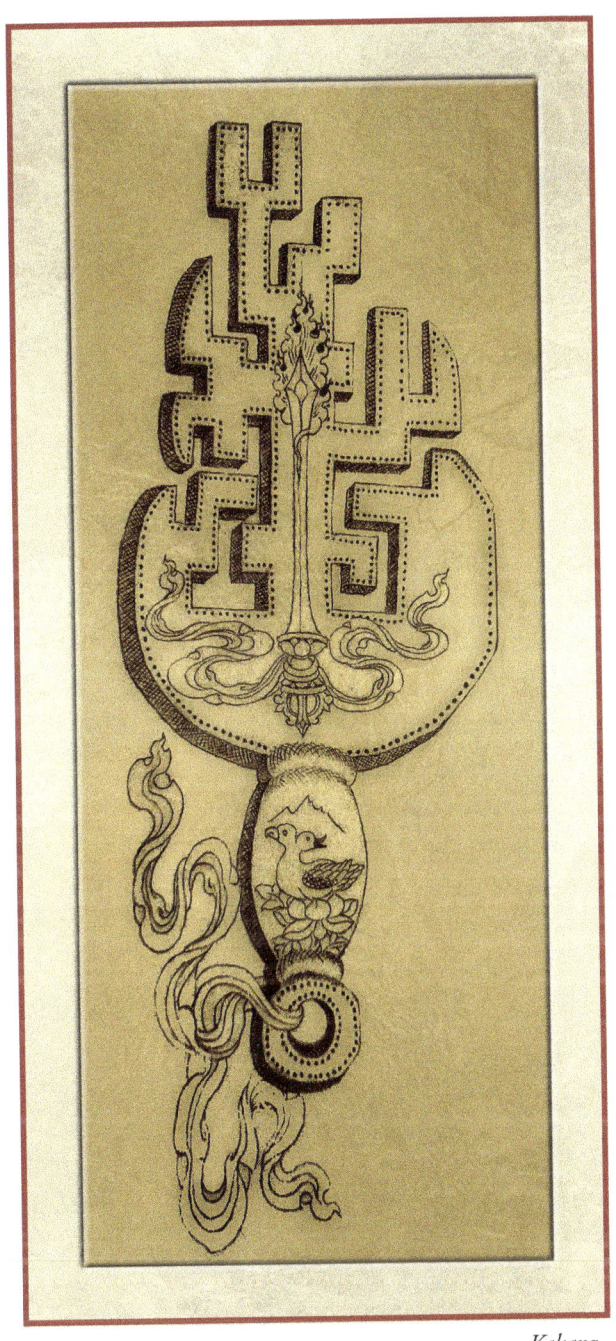

—Kalsang

The Kiss of the Vajra

Oh, my beloved,
Bathe in the radiant,
Divine, living light,
I the pristine of awareness
Effulgent in resplendent grace,
Living light of love.
Bathe, oh, my beloved,
As the clear light,
Flows from my crown,
Through my lips,
Bestowed, in unrelenting
Dharmadatu, unborn,
Never dying, this then is
The kiss of the Vajra.

Mortal Samsara

(dedicated to Namgay Dawa Rinpoche)

Bodhi leaves fall
On a single teardrop,
Turns the wheel
Of the *Dharma*.
One soul leaves,
One soul is born.
Bodhi leaves fall
On a single teardrop,
Turns the wheel.

Golden Buddha (replica of H.H. Dalai Lama's statues)
–Margaret Michie
Custom-made, 24 kt. gold,
Contact: margaretmichie99@gmail.com

The Golden Lotus

Emerging spontaneously
From my heart is the
Lotus of Golden Hue
With the name of my beloved
On it, transcending the
Oblivion of *Samsara*.
Amidst a shower of
Petals dyed in the
Enlightenment of the
Bodhisattvas,
Across the resplendent
Span of infinite Bodhicitta.

Sacred Kiss

In the tender, sweet
Softness of your kiss,
The mystery of love.
In love's revelation,
In all its sacred splendor,
Leaving samsara in
The dust of a bygone dream,
Vanishing as if there were no dreamer.
In your sacred kiss,
When bestowed in all
Triumph over delusions,
Longings and wounds turned
To ashes, when your lips,
In all humility,
Finally, in serene eloquence
Of the soul whose every breath
Chants my name in silence,
In the devotion of your heart,
Finally, as love blessed
Comes to us before I take
My last breath in this
Mortal coil, I would take
Death upon me willingly,
With your lips upon mine.
In the sacred union
Of co-mingled bliss.
In the action seal of
Karmamudra.

The Kiss of Everlasting Love

Betrothed to the *Dharmakaya*,
Neither longing, nor hunger
May overtake me,
But immeasurable grace falls
Upon my lips, as the great seal
In the splendor of the
Everlasting kiss.

Your Kiss of Liberation

Oh Beloved Consort
My heart trembles
In expectation.................
Oh, sacred are the lips
Where the nectar of
Immortality derive their
Taste from! Whence, I may
Know the love and lord
In divine union in all
Its supernal bliss,
Oh sacred is your kiss!

Buddhist Tantra

Where There Is Love

I will wait for you
At the edge of all worlds,
On the precipice of lost time,
On the back of the most
Revered angel,
Whose wings glorify heaven.
I will wait for you at dusk,
Where twilight never sleeps,
Where all hearts, frozen in time
From lovers lost,
Will now awaken to love
In the form of their beloved.
I will wait for you in *Dewachen*,
In worlds supernal,
In hell or heaven.
Not time, nor distance,
Nor forms of life can part us.
Where there is love
Between hearts there is sanctuary.
Where there is love
Between hearts there is destiny
Past the end of all the worlds.

Immortal Caress

With your lips upon mine,
Oh, beloved,
It is in your kiss,
The truth of love is tasted
For all time,
For liberation has
Dawned on your lips,
And in your arms,
In your embrace,
Will I lie in an eternity
That has awakened
To love and love alone
Where everything vanishes
Save Love.

Chakrasmvara in Union with Consort Vajravarahi
—Central Tibet 14th Century
—Rubin Museum of Himalayan Art

The Divine Kiss

The divine kiss of the *Vajra*,
The one taste from my lips
As love embraces itself,
It will reveal itself in my kiss.
And in the dream that dreams
Of itself in all of love divine,
You will have my love, beloved,
For the liberation of all mankind.
In the great expanse unending,
Wherever realms of life may be,
Whether samsara or nirvana,
I will never abandon thee.
No, I will never abandon thee,
For in the divine kiss of the *Vajra*,
Exulting, in the one taste from my lips,
As love supernal embraces itself,
This love, oh, my beloved, this love
Will reveal itself in our kiss.

Night of Love

We shall pierce the
Veil in tantric embrace.
Incarnations of our
Love have prepared us
For this night of splendour.
I will set thee aflame,
Lifetimes of sorrows hidden
Will vanish as if written on water.
The illusion of
Separation will adorn
oblivion in the ecstasy
of the Divine.
In this night of love
Oh Beloved,
In this night of love.

Chakrasamvara and Vajrayogini – 14th century Gilded statue Rubin Museum of Art

Tantric Yab Yum Tibetan

The Crown Tantric Embrace

In the great exaltation of union
Of wisdom and compassion
Primal purity reigns in the
Continuous display of luminosity
In effulgent light of bodhicitta
The everlasting ineffable radiant
Love ever present in the inner
Sanctum of the heart never dims
In tantric embrace all disappears
Save the profound essence,
In such love I embrace thee
Beloved for all time to come.

Of Sorrows and Joys Taken

Let my love linger
Upon your lips,
In the divine presence
Of the *Mahamudra*.
Then, there will be
No need to speak
To me of love,
For its knowing will be
In our kiss, the path
Of sorrows and joys taken.
A single tear winds its way
Through many causes and effects,
Our hearts connected
To all living beings,
In the splendor of *Bodhicitta*.

The Mala of Love

It is your *mala*,
Which is strung
Around my throat.
Your *mala*,
Which your fingers caressed,
Through years of practice,
Like the holy beads of *Bodhicitta*,
Nestled in my heart
In unsurpassed love.
Your *mala*, strung
Around my throat
As devotion for
The liberation of all
Sentient beings
In your love
Forever.

In the Splendour of Love

In the splendour of love,
The one taste is not manifest,
The one taste is not hidden,
The one taste is not revealed,
Nor is it unrevealed.
Seen with the one eye,
Not seen with the two,
In regal embrace,
In the splendour of love.

Chakrasamvara/Vajrayogini 15th-16th century bronze sculpture from Nepal

You Will Drink My Tears

My tears fall on your cheeks,
Enchanted by your true love,
The crown of which reflects
All sentient beings.
Oh, my beloved love,
Oh, beloved,
Your foresworn promise
Upon beholding my first tears
As you kiss my lips
A trembling, after long years.
Where heaven's first cause is that of
Love never failing,
In all its sweet
And tender embrace.
That I love you, oh, my dearest,
Above even heaven's grace,
Where immortals reside
In enraptured embrace,
Here, you will drink my tears,
As holy nectar illuminating
All of endless space.

The Kiss of Liberation

The kiss of liberation,
Luminosity, radiant
In the empty expanse
Where the lips meet;
So does the heart of
Supernal bliss,
For the sake of all
Sentient beings.

Prajñāpāramitā Devī and Mañjuśrī in yab yum

My Beloved Love

Oh, my beloved love,
In radiant grace
Thou hast found my lips,
At long last in tantric bliss,
Where the one taste exists,
Where there are no
Sentient beings,

No *samsara*,
No *nirvana*.
Only the one taste in my lips
In the ecstatic embrace
Of the beloved.

By Love Alone

Oh, my beloved love,
Come. There is only
Love here waiting for
You, in the embrace
Of *Rigpa*, the infinite
Grace of *Mahamudra*.
Only love, and by love alone
Is the cloudless sky,
The emptiness of the void,
Which truly is never empty,
The existential bliss of
Awareness itself.

By love alone are we not born.
By love alone we do not die.
The same root is the story of love,
So, come, my beloved,
And know the one taste in
Love's luminosity,
In the sacred heart of love.

For As Long as I Shall Live

Oh, my dearest, for as long
As I shall live, through all of
My incarnations in every form,
For as long as I shall die,
Through the *bardos* of life and death,
I shall love you as my beloved.
For the sake of all,
For the sake of love itself,
For I have become the very love
I have sought in such immeasurable grace,
So, now, beloved, I can do naught else
But love you in the radiance
Of the *Dharmakaya*
That itself is naught else but love.

Oh, My Beloved

Oh, my beloved,
Amongst all beloveds,
In the heart of the
Dharmakaya, I wait.
Oh, my truest love,
Amongst all true loves,
In the heart of radiant
Bliss, I wait.
Oh, my spiritual consort,
Amongst all consorts,
I place my mala around
Your throat, and through
Beginning-less time
We have made aspirations
For the liberation of sentient beings.
All I dedicate to you.
Oh, my beloved,
Amongst all beloveds,
Rest in my embrace.

Oldest Tibetan painting

In the Embrace of Bodhicitta

And as Bodhicitta
falls from my lips,
commingling with yours—
the fragrant nectar
of supernal bliss—
as the
Amrita of luminous love
tastes supreme,
in this tender, pristine
moment of our kiss,
in Rigpa's embrace,
in this paradise of the Holy,
the glorious pillar
of living, radiant light—
the breath of love—
flows as a river
of illumination.

As all phenomena
disappears,
Bodhicitta
ever blossoms—

in sanctity,
the veil has dissolved
in the splendour of
self-arising, spontaneous awareness,
in the ever-present splendour of love.

Samarasya

You have taken
my tears
as your very own,
as I have taken yours.
They are gifts
between us,
in shared longing,
in shared trust.
I know you will
never abandon
nor betray our love,
for it is the light
between your brows—
this bright illumination
that is your soul,
I have loved for so long.
Long, long before I ever
even knew your name.
And I know, dearest, I know,
when you take my hand
and clasp it firmly in yours,
all of the weight of

my sorrows disappear,
and I know,
I have not lived this life in vain.
It is this love between us
that allows
our flesh to become
the transparent radiance
of the Living Light.
As self-awareness dawns
in simultaneous bliss,
and our kiss blazes forth
the celestial birth of stars—
shattering the illusion
of separation,
for the enlightenment
of all sentient beings.
I rest in your arms,
dedicating our love—
nothing less than love
in supernal awakening.

Oldest 1800's Thankgha Samantabhadri

Consort

May the wheel of the Dharma turn
When we make love, as the
Union is not for my sake alone
Nor for your sake alone
But for the sake of all sentient
Beings, for I have come into
This world to love you and you alone.
In all of the realms I will, beloved,
Love you unto and beyond death
The secret you will taste from my
Lips, even in the last kiss, will reveal
The great seal in such tenderness
That loneliness will vanish from
Your heart forever even after
I am gone and
You must walk alone.

With No Regrets

My soul cries out in an empathy,
In the one river all humanity drinks from,
For all of the sufferings of all
Beings in all of the realms,
Wherever there is sentient life throughout,
My soul doth cry out.
How can I liken my love for thee?
As my beloved resides in my heart
For all of eternity in the void,
Which is not empty, but effulgent
With a love never born and never dying.
Forgiveness and compassion are one.
The veil of delusion vanishes.
My heart becomes the unending
Essence of life itself. The river of
Forgetfulness overflows, and I am
Brought to my knees in blazing light.
My soul, in the great expanse,
Surrenders to loving you.

At the end of the end,
What is fate if not love?
What is my love for you,

If not the destiny of mankind?
What wrongs I have done thee,
I will bear the responsibility.
I will eat the ashes of my heart,
In solemn, silent cry, to supplicate
The heavens in a devotional plea
To not sacrifice the love that I bear thee.
How I must have failed thee!
How I must have betrayed thee,
Memories buried in *samskaras*,
The burning pain of eviscerating
Tears having a life of their own.
These tears, fully aware,
These tears,
Upon knowing the hurt
I must have caused
In prior incarnation is unbearable.
If by grace in this long journey of
Many lifetimes where we have loved,
If by grace I may help heal thy wounds,
If by grace I am nothing but love to thee,
Having found you again in *samsaric* realms,
Having traversed both hell and heaven to do so,
If, by grace, you can find comfort in my love,
I will go to my grave with no regrets.

The Respite of Rigpa

The thorn in my heart,
Lifetimes of such love.
Only *Dakinis* are qualified to understand.
The only respite is *Rigpa*.
Oh, my beloved,
Whose embrace is the
Crown of the *Dharmakaya*.
Oh, my beloved,
Whose tears I weep.

Chakrasmvara with Consort Vajravarahi
Kham Provence, Eastern Tibet 19th Century
–Rubin Museum of Himalayan Art

Bodhicitta Rises

Bodhicitta knows all sorrows.
It has walked beside me
Through lifetimes of sufferings
Bodhicitta was with me,
When my feet splintered as
Shards of broken glass, ribbons
Of red crying out for oblivion,
In the wasteland of deluded dreams.
In the thousand, thousand forgotten
Lifetimes of meetings, a thousand,
Thousand lifetimes of separations
Bodhicitta has never left me.

Kneeling beside my pain it has held me
So I would not shatter nor truly be alone.

To stand naked, resolute, in our own suffering,
As our wounds open like Luminous, self aware,
Glittering points of light. Here Bodhicitta is born,
In the very heart of pain, here compassion is born,
Here, at the very edge of the abyss—
The threshold of annihilation,

Bodhicitta rises,
Knowing all sorrows,
Embracing all beings,
Endlessly without end . . .
As the heart cracks wide open
And suffering is touched
By grace,
We recognize, the truth,
Of love.

For M

My heart trembles at the thought of your suffering.
I cannot bear it. Let me carry your burden—
I will do so gladly.
For it is in your loving me
that I can bear all sorrows,
shouldering them as though I were
the helpmeet of humanity.
I will wear your love and your pain
as armor,
as a shield,
as an adornment and testimony—
jeweled with wounds transformed
into the divine transcendence of
luminous, exalted grace.
For, if I must suck the poison
from your eviscerating points of darkened light,
crying out for release,
as if you have fallen
from the Shekinah above Keter,
denied by your own shadow,
I will be there.
Even if all the worlds are against you,
I shall never leave you, beloved.

Never shall I leave you.
My love remains yours.
It is my pledge to you,
long before the worlds were birthed.
There is surely an end to sorrow.
There is no end to love.

I Wait

So, beloved, I wait
As the morning star,
My shorn wings,
Whose wounds give meaning
To humanity's suffering.
Beloved, I wait
Where there is no waiting,
Only love's calling to itself,
As the foundation and
Crown of the Dharmakaya.
I know you will even
Embrace my scars.

Tantric Vajrayana

The Nostalgia of Nirvana

Blood stains my tears.
Orchids thought dead
Bloom overnight.
The nostalgia of Nirvana
In your kiss.

True Loves First Kiss

Unstained, in radical
Compassion..... even,
When I left this mortal
Coil, as I have,
So many times before
I never forgot your love,
Even when I crossed
The great river of forgetfulness.
Never, oh my beloved,
Have I forgotten your love.

Mandala Guru Rinpoche –Anna Lieb-Dubino

The Crown of the Dharmakaya

In such love,
How may sorrow exist?
Sorrow does not exist
In such love,
Sorrow does not exist,
Has never existed,
And will not exist
In such love,
May every sentient being
Awaken to this love,
The crown of the *Dharmakaya*,
The love where there
Is no sorrow.

Your Mala of Love

It is your love
Strung around my throat,
Your mala of bodhicitta
Strung around my heart,
Your mala of devotion.
I will not forget you,
Never, even if I must go to my death
Without your hand in mine.
Your mala forever embraces me
In unsurpassed love.
Oh, beloved,
It is your love
Strung around my throat
That has given me the speech
Of the divine mantra of liberation
As loves final mystery.

Buddhist Tonglen

Oh, let me not suffer for my sake alone,
When I utter this desolate, mournful,
Fragile cry of eviscerating tears,
So bleak and lonely in torment.
When I cry this sound of suffering
Unbearable at its root of ignorance,
When even being a corpse will not
Free me from this pain,
Let it be. Let it be the last sound,
The final, unutterable cry
Of humanity's sorrows, their angst,
Their pain, their despair.
Let it be their last.

Skull Inner Offerings —Anna Lieb-Dubino

Crown of Skulls

Hidden behind the fallen blossoms,
Whose fragrance of love
Guides me in solitude,
Is the secret of all sufferings.
I accept all the gifts sorrow brings,
Alone on this path I tread,
Solitary, in a boat made of glass.
Transparent are the karmas
We must endure.
Barefoot, I make the crossing
Of the great ocean of samsara,
Without beginning or ending.
On the far shore,
There you will find me wearing
A crown of skulls, naked,
Now adorned in
The radiance of liberation.

Death and Impermanence

Death and impermanence,
Shadow of my shadow
In loving kindness, always,
Do not waste a moment.
The unfailing karmic laws
Of cause and effect cease not,
Crossing the great ocean,
Always in loving kindness.
Always in *Bodhicitta*.
Then, death and impermanence
Matter not.

Effulgent in the Grace

Across space and time, my *mala* of love
I place around your neck for all of
Your countless incarnations.
May it be beloved.
May it be that your soul has found sanctuary
Until we meet again.
Oh, noble love,
The great mystical display rests
In a single teardrop, which contains
Every hope and fervent wish
Of all of mankind,
And even so this love, this love,
The *Dakinis* regard as sacred.

Bodhicitta

The Love that remains when
The lover and beloved vanish
In the Union which surpasses,
Is, without cause and effect
In radiant illumination,
Before all worlds
And after the great Pralaya,
Is Bodhicitta.

Mystere —Albert Bolk

The Cloudless Sky

Tong pa Nyid.
Rest, where skeletons dance
In non-duality.
Rest, in pure presence,
Where the dead may dance
In the cloudless sky.

The Kiss of the Dakinis

Upon the lips of every mortal
Upon the lips of every immortal
The kiss of liberation alights
as destiny unfolds, there is no
place else to go but home.
Crossing the great ocean,
blessed with the Dharma,
the taste of love
in its infinite embrace
calls us home
to the citadel of
Supreme Bodhicitta

Surrender to Love

I drink my own tears
As I drink my own blood,
Throughout cycles of birth,
Throughout cycles of death,
Cascades of vanishing
Thoughts in aeonic moments of delusions
Rife with the agony of projected wounds
Suffused in utter madness, this
Collective matrix of torments
Common to us all,
Vanquished in the stillness in
The sacred palace of awareness
As its light dawns as my very own.
Oh humanity!
Slay what must be slain!
Rest, rest in the equipoise
Of the temple of your own mind.
Rest in the love that surpasses
The illusion of birth and death.
Surrender to love.

In the Essence of Tonglen

I beheld the Love
that embraces all—
great and small.

I opened my veins
in the charnel ground,
where even death itself
dares not remain.

Each vein imbued
with the light that never dims,
each vein a strand of the heart,
flooded with the tears
of the shadow's projection—
a deluded self,
illusory yet seeming real.

As the Light excoriated my wounds,
which never truly belonged to me,
a thousand sorrows melted into dawn.

The flame blazed forth from my heart
to all sentient beings—
annihilated was the shadow,
annihilated was the torment;
only Love remained.
And in that boundless stillness,
the breath of all worlds
rose and fell as one.
And only love remained.

Chod

Amongst the bleached and silent bones,
I sat in the echo of mind's stillness there,
I listened to the shadows of the spirits,
And the corpses of all the realms did dance,
And I sang, I sang the song of liberation.
The spirits drew near, the dead did dance,
There I was in the echo of mind's resting.
As I welcomed all, those of the darkness
Who sought to torture my mind
Did I welcome as friends
And my blood we did drink
In the skullcup of love.

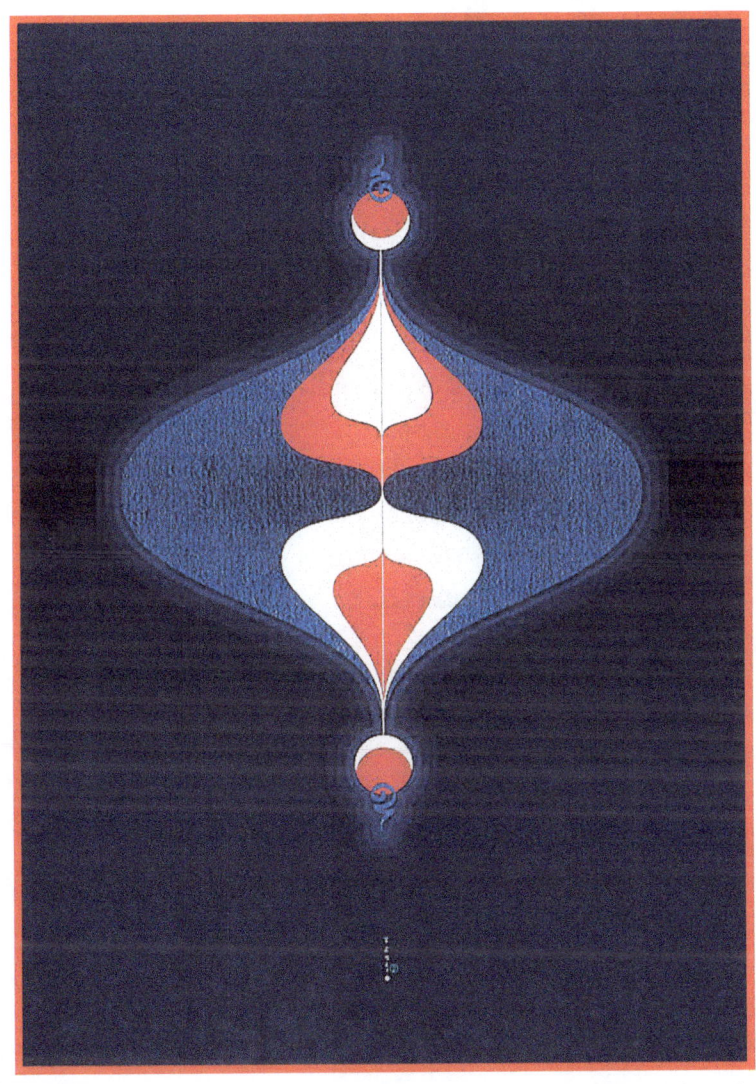

Turiya —Mark-Kusek

Accoutrements

Death and life
Have become one
In radiant luminosity,
The exalted awareness
In the citadel of primordial light,
The transfiguration,
The perceived, conditioned
Sense of an autonomous self
With all its accoutrements
Of karmas, *samskaras*,
Gone, gone, gone.

The Heart of Forgiveness

Who amongst us
Has not suffered
For love?
The path is narrow
And steep.
The sacrifices made
Are but adornments
In eternal liberation. For,
What lay in the heart of love
Is forgiveness.

Ancient Chinese Bodhisattva

Blessed Garment of Love

I will love you dearest
With my very last breath,
Your love, imprinted on
My own samskaras,
Inked on my own aggregates
And worn on my own soul.
Your love has never left me
Through so many lifetimes.
It will accompany me through
the Bardos of life and death,
And I will wear your love
Even throughout my karmas,
In eons gone and to come,
As the blessed garment of Love.

The Kiss of the Dharmakaya

All poisons of this world,
All sorrows,
All wounds,
All grieving and grief,
All partings and meetings,
All love that has been forgotten,
All love remembered,
All
In the kiss of the *Dharmakaya*.
Oh, my beloved love,
In the kiss that lasts forever,
All
Healed in radiant bliss.

Tantric Love -Ancient India

Tantric Goddess Rajasthan

Never for My Sake Alone

May my swollen tears that bleed humanity's
Samsaric delusions, so spiritually crippled,
Let it be my tears, my unrelenting pain that vanquishes all
For every sentient being in any realm.
Let it be that my hell, my torture, my rebirths
Vanquish all; and in that last gasp of
Immortal pain, the hope of humanity is born
In the recognition of the one blessed taste.
In one song, in a unison that recognizes
All sentient beings as one, in a love of such
Undimmable light that all worlds, in one
Exquisite moment, all beings are relieved
Of all sufferings, and only know true joy.
My suffering, may it be of value for all
Sentient beings in non-linear time.
This suffering on the wheel
Within the wheel of all time
That not death, nor rebirth, will
Release me from. But may it heal and liberate
Every sentient being, may I have not borne
Suffering for myself alone, but for all.
Oh, let me not suffer for my sake alone,
Never for my sake alone.

Utterly Beyond

Utterly beyond
Birth and death,
The jeweled crown
Of liberation,
The ineffable mirror,
The radiance
Of clear light,
The lustre of which
Is the playground
Of the *dakinis* and *dacas*
Come dance with me
In freedom absolute,
In the love that will
Never fail thee.

Blessings

Blessed are the children of light.
Blessed are the children of darkness.
Blessed are the fallen angels.
Blessed are those who have reaped
What they sow. Blessed are they
Who have survived the apocalypse
In the abyss of their own delusions,
For all are on the journey home.

The End of Samsara

Enduring endless rebirths,
I have come to the end of
The wilderness of samsara,
As I stand on the precipice
Of liberation, in strong faith,
In authenticity, the dharma,
Ever leads me onwards.
With such devotion as the
Guiding light of my soul,
There is no need to ask,
No need to know how long
The journey may take.

Healing Mandala –Mark-Kusek

Yab Yum Kuntuzangpo Samantrabhadra –Anna Lieb-Dubino

Sacred Kiss of Liberation

In your sacred kiss upon
My lips I thought long since
Turned to stone,
In your sacred kiss upon
My lips, where the blood coursing
Through my veins I thought
Long since had become
Poison to my soul.
With all the karmas in delusion's
Web of lies I have believed,
It was in your kiss, beloved,
It was in your kiss
That I was finally released.
Liberation dawned, beloved.
Liberation dawned in your kiss.
In your kiss was I released
From *Samsara's* cage,
Imprisoned in my own illusion,
Imprisoned by my own lies.
Now, the truth of love
Has been tasted for all time
In the one taste, beloved,
In the one taste sublime.

The Mala of Radiant Love

Each precious bead on
My Mala is eloquent
With your sacred love
Each bead, I wrap
My fingers around.
Each bead radiates such
Love as a human may bear.
Unforgettable is the moment
Where the singularity of
Loves essence was
Realized and a divine
Tear fell removing all
Obscurations.

A Garland of Bodhicitta

Love adorns in resplendence.
In the heart of forgiveness,
Come, drink from this well,
Whose source has no beginning,
And no ending.
Come and share the waters of love!
All you can bear will be given to you,
As long as you share.
Come, wear this garland of *bodhicitta*,
And know no more sorrow.

A Single Lamp Is Lit

In this mortal world
Of partings
A single lamp is lit.
Its flame embraces
The eternal exquisite
Moment of the love
Which endures through
All time and forms,
Remembering nothing
Lasts forever but love.

Mirror, Lucid

Upon the garland of lifetimes liberated,
I stamped the image
Never-ending of my beloved,
Whose mirror, lucid,
Revealed every moment's
Love in grace;
And in the clarity
Of exulted empty space,
Where wisdom's
Awareness knows no veil,
My love for you is as
The dawning of *Dharmakaya* itself,
The great unborn,
Uncreated expanse of love eternal,
Where even death holds no sway.

Turiya the Mirror –Dzogchen painting
–Anna Lieb-Dubino

No End to Bodhicitta

Oh immeasurable *Bodhicitta!*
Of eons, endless in supernal light!
The heart is the mirror sacred!
In wisdom's grace. Oh beloved!
Harken to the voice of love.
Know there is an end
To pain, beloved,
I promise you,
There is no end
To *Bodhicitta*.

Far Better

Far, far better would it be
To go through
The dark night of the soul,
Than to submit
To samsara.
Far better would it be
To work with one's
Illusory shadow
Than to surrender
To samsara.
Far better to awaken
To immeasurable love,
No matter how great the journey.

Tsakli Vajrayogin –Anna Lieb-Dubino

Mamo Ekajati

I am the non dual queen.
I am the smoke that arises
from the funeral pyre.
I vanquish the demons
Of your own mind, assailing
Enemies within and without.
As the great guardian with
My single eye,
I set you free from bondage.
When you are left alone,
Cast aside, when you have
Nothing left
The sharp blade of my love
Will set you free.
I have no equal.

Mantra of Liberation

The perceived self,
Individuated, separate
From the source
Is liberated, the veil
Vanishing in the true
Light of everlasting love,
Fully cognizant, aware,
Bodhicitta itself resplendent.

–Anna Lieb-Dubino

The Secret Language

The secret language of the heart,
Upon understanding,
Reveals the illusion of karma.

Only Love

In the magical display of illusion,
Where the dead may dance,
And all phenomena vanish,
Only love never ceases to be.

White Tara

In the Merciful Cathedral

Deep within your own heart,
no chain of sorrows binds.
As grasping dies,
pure essence doth impart.
The lotus breathes
its life eternal, as rise it must—
born in unveiled, luminous trust.
Obscurations disappear,
vanishing in the reality
of the embrace of endless love,
vanishing in the
clear light of love.
And in every moment, a trembling—
in everything that lives and dies,
the wheel no longer may turn
in the stable, quiet, forgiving mind.
For no more chains of sorrow will there be,
as all grasping dies
to bind the loving heart—
to bind
the Loving heart.

For the Sake of All Beings

I love you—
not for my sake alone,
but for the sake
of all sentient beings.

O, how do I love thee still,
after so many lifetimes and karmas?
The answer lies
in the very heart
of the living light
of love everlasting—
the mystery of all mysteries,
the longing of every heart
that has ever yearned to love,
not for one's sake alone.

O Beloved,
when we make love,
as becoming and co-mingling
of radiant awareness,
the birth of all worlds
resides in this sacred act—
in the supernal bliss
of the Great Seal.

Through the seal of karmamudrā,
we have become
the love we sought—
the love we would
live and die for,
for the sake
of all sentient beings.

Yab Yum Heruka Consort –Anna Lieb-Dubino

Only Love Is Not Written on Water

If I have taken my love for you—
as mother,
as wife,
as husband,
as brother—
in the kiss that lasts forever...
If I have taken my love for you
As the divine mantle
Of Mahāmudrā,

If I have loved you
for the sake of all sentient beings,
in whatever form or realm
they dwell—

Then I will have no regrets.

For only love
is not written on water.

O Let Me Be the Salvation

O let me be the salvation,
the healer of all your wounds.
For I am the Love you have sought
across unbearable cycles of lifetimes—
the Love that beareth all burdens,
the Love that is the very heart-essence
of even the void.
For I am Bodhicitta,
the inherent momentum
before and after the great Pralaya,
before your lips utter even a prayer.
I have never been born,
I have never died.
I reside in your veins and bones,
in the secret space between your atoms,
where light remembers itself as Love.
In the still point beyond becoming,
I am the motion, of all worlds
the silent vow of every awakened heart.
Through your tears I flow as mercy—
oh, you must understand...
When your own soul remembers

its infinite face,
when you bow in surrender,
all suffering dissolves
like salt in the ocean of awareness.
And in the ineffable radiance
of the living light of love
I love you.
And you will know this Love
as the Love that resides
as the only law:
as Light remembering itself
as Love.
As the love
you really are.

Vajra Chain

Like a garland of pristine pearls,
This *Vajra* chain,
Luminous in the sound of ah,
Luminosity arising,
The nature of the mind,
Free with no grasping,
Free from delusion,
Free from suffering.
The one taste beyond
Nirvana, beyond *Samsara*.
Beloved, rest.
Oh, my beloved,
Rest in such love that love
Itself is born of and never dies.

Flower Garland Red Bliss Queen, Tantra Dechen Gyalmo
—Anna Lieb-Dubino

The Garland of Empty Space

I do dwell in noble array
Within the sacred palace of my skull.
Oh, light supernal of bliss,
Where mind and heart have
Become one.
Oh, light supernal of all souls,
Reside in the light of lights,
Wherein my heart has become
The refuge of all who suffer
In the garland of empty space.

Cherish Love

As dawn breaks over
An infinitude of worlds,
Where phenomena and habitual
Tendencies seem to be reality,
And the mind obscured
By residual karmas is at unrest.
Remember, above all else,
Cherish love, the nectar
Of everlasting Bodhicitta
Residing within you.
Let the phenomena you perceive as
Real be an offering
On the altar of love.

The Red Drop or Bindu: Tigle of primordial female wisdom
—Anna Lieb-Dubino

Abiding

Abiding in non-dual
awareness,
Where compassion is
the splendorous crown
of the Dharmadhātu,

And I—
a single drop
of the love of Bodhicitta—
dissolve.

No longer separate,
the seeing and the seen
become one.

I abide,

And in abiding,
I vanish,
yet I am more

Present
than ever.

The One Taste

Oh, my beloved,
Taste the one holy taste with me,
Beyond all sorrows,
Beyond all concepts,
In exquisite embrace.
Oh, my beloved,
Taste the one taste with me.
We are liberated
Into the *Dharmakaya*
For the sake of all sentient beings.
Pristine, primordial
Amrita ascends
Through the channel,
And the sense of I is obliterated.
Only the truest love
Is now fully cognizant,
Spontaneously accomplishing
For the benefit of all
Through the great compassion,
Never-wavering *Dharmakaya*.

This is the unity of appearance
And emptiness,
Accomplished in supreme
Arousal of *Bodhicitta*
For the sake of all sentient beings.
Oh, my beloved,
For the sake of all sentient beings,
In the clear light of
The one taste.

Oh Beloved

I adore you as no other,
In the radiant heart of
Bodhicitta, all THINGS
Are fulfilled for
The sake of all
Sentient beings.
Yet, I adore you
As I adore no other,
For you are
My beloved.

The Lamp to Guide the Way

The Light of Love—everlasting,
never grows dim.
The vessel you thought
shattered beyond repair,
the broken, eviscerated,
tormented heart—reborn!

Come, sip the waters
of the Dharmadhātu.
Just one moment
of true love—
just the one tear
you shed when compassion
awakens in pristine awareness—

Just one tear,
and aeons of obscurations
dissolve like mist
before the dawn.

In that silence,
the lamp within all beings
flares forth—
guiding the way home.

The Purpose of Love

In the purpose of love,
Impermanence may not be grasped.
It is in the self-liberation
Of all phenomena
That everything appears,
Yet nothing endures
Of solitary presence.
Yet, in the ineffable,
Living light of love,
It never dies.
As the mantra of liberation,
The perceived self,
Individual, separate
From the source
Is liberated, the veil,
Vanishing in the true light
Of everlasting love,
Fully cognizant, aware,
Bodhicitta itself resplendent.

Until My Last Breath
(heart sentence of Namgay Dawa Rinpoche)

Until my last breath,
Of all of the breaths I will breathe
In all of my incarnations,
In whatever form they will take,
I will work tirelessly for the
Liberation of all sentient beings.
Until all have crossed over the
Great ocean of samsara,
Until all know true joy.
Until my last breath,
May my heart never falter
From the true love
Love can bear
Until my last breath.

On the Altar of Love

The vault of Heaven has opened.
Numerous stars embrace each other.
Love has formed all things,
And as evening tide sets in
Across the universe,
All of life teems with *Bodhicitta*,
Resounding in our kiss,
Our kiss, beloved,
We have offered
On the altar of love.

Samantabhadra

Of Rigpa

The first kiss of true awareness,
Exalted as the crown of *Rigpa*,
Needs no adulation nor belief,
As oblivion no longer exists.
One cannot speak of *Rigpa*
Without speaking of love.
My tears fall on your cheeks,
Enchanted by your true love,
The crown of which reflects
All sentient beings.

Oh Great Primordial Liberation!

Oh, great primordial liberation!
Free of conceptual beliefs
Free of grasping thoughts
As phenomena become the
Adornments in the Dharma,
And Love, in the equipoise of
Freedom and kindness rule.

17th century White Tara

What Is Love?

What is love,
Oh, my beloved,
If not for the sake
Of all sentient beings?
As love loves itself
In all, everlasting,
Luminous guise aware,
Beloved, aware in
Sacred tender stillness,
Where tears have no more
Necessity to weep.
But in the hearts of all,
The endless embrace of love
Reigns supreme,
Across withering *samsaric* delusion,
Where all is written on water,
Save only love.
Only love lasts, and only love
Will conquer all,
Far, far beyond the grave.

Crown of Endless Luminosity

Here, the delusion of
Nihilism vanishes.
Remain, beloved,
In the equipoise of
The crystal clarity,
Drinking the nectar
Of ego's oblivion.
Rest, rest free,
Free, free from the wheel,
Free of hope,
Free from fear,
In the endless,
Never-born luminosity of love.

Surrender

There is no past
There is no future,
There is only the
Surrender to Bodhicitta

'Though Its Very Essence

'Though its very essence
Is unborn,
It gives life to all,
Beyond eternal.
It cannot be annihilated,
It is, oh, my beloved,
The very love we all
Have sought over and over
Through far too many cycles
Of sorrows,
Yet, it has never left us.
This love is,
The seal of *Mahamudhra*
Let us realize the
One taste in
Co-emergent bliss.

No One's Blood

I offer no one's blood
But my own, no one's
Heart but my own.
I offer no one's flesh.
I eat no corpse.
I make no corpse of
Any living being,
I sacrifice no one,
No one else.
I offer all my own delusions
On the threshold of liberation,
Resting in equipoise, where
The bliss of sacred awareness
Conjoins with calm abiding
In divine love.
There is no need
To cause harm
To any being,
To live or to die.

Shangpa White Khechari (Kachod Karmo) – 18th century Tibetan thangka

Unfathomable Love

In the dawning
of the spontaneous awareness—
the luminous, uncontrived Rigpa,
Love will not abandon thee—
not now,
not ever.
Even in the silence of *Sūnyatā*,
even in the shadow of delusion
Love abides.
It is this *Prakāśa*—
the pristine light
that neither falters
nor fades;
the *Svabhāva* essence
that remembers you
beyond all forgetting,
beyond the veils of samsara,
beyond the grasp of ego's illusion.
This is the *Maitrī*—
unconditional, unfathomable Love,
the Dharmakāya's eternal embrace,
awakening the buddha-nature

that is ever-present—
never diminishing,
never grasping—
but is the love
beyond all sorrow.
This, is how I love you.

The Garland of Bodhicitta

Come! Let us live in
The citadel of primordial
Awareness, where there is
No perceiver nor perception.
Here, our garland of
Bodhicitta reaches across
Delusion, and vajras dance
In realms of light
As the sense of I vanishes,
And all that remains
Is *Bodhicitta*,
Liberation's permanent exaltation.

–Kalsang

This Crown of Love

The first kiss of true awareness,
Exalted as the crown of *Rigpa*,
Needs no adulation nor belief.
This crown of love,
Radiant, ineffable, incandescent,
Beyond eternal, immaculate,
In spontaneous presence,
The essence of which is love.
Beloved, I devote my heart
To the liberation of all
Sentient beings,
The crown of which is of love,
And endureth for all time.

O Belovèd

O Belovèd,
'tis the Dream
dreaming itself,
the breath within a breath,
a sigh within the heartbeat of the stars.

O what doth lie
behind the veil of vanishing forms,
beyond the rise and fall of lifetimes' tide?
Only Love—
only Love abideth still.

When all the worlds do fade to mist,
and every name is but an echo,
Love remaineth, tender,
holding all in gentle flame.

So rest, my heart, in that still sea,
where time need not turn its page;
for Love alone, and evermore,
doth cradle all eternity.

Buddha –Kalsang

The Ecstasy of Love

The scent of your soul
has seduced me
through the portals
of life and death,
death and life—

in and out
of the flesh of disguise,
as woman or man,
formless beneath form.

No one may touch me
but you—
not merely in body,
but in the deep ache
of remembrance,

the vow carried
across lifetimes,
whispered in dreams,
etched into silence.

And through you—
only you—
the destiny of humankind
is fulfilled
in the final ecstasy of love.

Not the flame that burns,
but the light that remains.

In the Stillness Deep

All that is of love
will never die.

Seemingly eternal
is the morphic field of saṃsāra—
so deeply habitual
the delusory sense
of a separate self,

Perceived
again and again
in non-linear time,
grasping for survival,
clinging to its own
neurotic perception.

Karmas,
saṃskāras,
vṛttis,
aggregates—
rippling echoes
in the stream of becoming.

And yet—

In stillness deep,
in the calm abiding
of heart and mind aligned,
in the radiant luminosity
of the living light of love—
is your true inheritance:

The freedom
from the cage of thoughts
we have believed.

Here,
in the stillness deep,
in the stillness
deep.

Beloved Consort

In the singularity
Of the moment
Of awareness,
In the embrace
Of divine love,
When reincarnation
And fate become
Adornments, I wait
For you, as consort.
This moment between
Us beloved, is worth
My life
And death.

Eternal Love Couple – Hindu painting

Dorje Chang Yab Yum and Consort –Anna Lieb-Dubino

For the Love of Rigpa

In noble heart I do dwell
Past the *kalpas*,
Past the *yugas*.
All life is contained within.
There is no without.
Dakinis and *dacas* know
My name, singing the song
Of liberation for all of those
Who have ears to listen,
And the heart to love.
All suffering is wiped out.
Only *Bodhicitta* is known here.
You have become the precious
Jewel you have sought in
Timeless awareness,
In the noble embrace of *Rigpa*,
Where love reigns supreme.

How May I Liken My Love for Thee

How may I liken my love for thee?
As in the mystical union of the Divine—
the invisible movements
of the infinite world of illumination.

Thy presence is the raging flame
that burns within my own heart,
giving life to all, saving none;
the very reason Love,
in all its infinite tenderness and grace,
embraces the plentitude of all worlds.

It is here, God remembers itself
in its ineffable illumination

In thee, I behold the secret pulse
of stars becoming light—
the longing of eternity
to be seen within thy gaze.

When thou art near,
I tremble;
I cannot contain
the love I have for thee.

Separation falls away,
the corridors of time vanish,
and Love—Love alone—
becomes all that remains.

As the heavens dissolve
in the radiance of our union,
the *Dharmakāya*
tastes itself through us.

The sublime, ineffable *Ein Sof Ohr*
resumes its purpose.

For I do know this truth:
to love thee, by my soul's own measure,
is to awaken
to the Divine Itself—

A love so deep,
no mortal heart can bear it alone,
save by the grace
of Love's own mercy.

Kadak

Oh Luminous Mind of
Love everlasting,
You are the supreme self
The unborn Buddha nature,
You are always present,
Making all things possible.
Yet veiled by delusion
Yet unseen by karmas,
When revealed stainless
In pure knowing, the heart,
Can do naught else but
Love in radical kindness.
This is the legacy of all
Things that are born and die
In the end and the beginning
There is only your light in love
You are pure holy compassion,
Your radiant Light every sentient
Being will eventually see as
The Light of their own soul...

Ḍākinī Maṇḍala - Dudjom Rinpoche's Khandro'i Thugtig

Khandro'i Thugthig, 'Ḍākinī's Heart Essence', which is more fully known as 'The Treasury of Accomplishments: The Practice of the Profound Path of the Ḍākinī [Yeshe Tsogyal]' is the main ḍākinī practice of the Dudjom Tersar lineage, and one of the four main terma cycles of Dudjom Rinpoche, who revealed it as a mind treasure or gongter in 1928.

The exquisite painting shows a typical form of ḍākinī maṇḍala with a single door to enter the sacred feminine realm of pleasurable sensation, joyful experiences and great bliss transcending ordinary pleasure and bliss as it unfolds in the vast open dimension of its empty aspect.

From the Caṇḍamahāroṣaṇatantram:
Women are heaven, women are the Dharma,
And women are truly the supreme austerity.
Women are the Buddha, women are the Saṅgha,
Women are the Perfection of Wisdom.
striyaḥ svargaḥ striyo dharmaḥ striya eva paraṃ tapaḥ |
striyo buddhaḥ striyaḥ saṅghaḥ prajñāpāramitā striyaḥ || 8. 14

བུད་མེད་མཐོ་རིས་བུད་མེད་ཆོས། །
བུད་མེད་དེ་ཉིད་དཀའ་ཐུབ་མཆོག །
སངས་རྒྱས་བུད་མེད་དགེ་འདུན་ཉིད། །
བུད་མེད་ཤེས་རབ་ཕར་ཕྱིན་ཉིད། །

For a woman, the man is a deity;
For a man, the woman is a deity.
They should honor each other
By uniting the vajra and the lotus.
strīṇāṃ ca pumān devo devatā strī narasya hi |
anyonyaṃ bhavet pūjā vajrapadmaprayogataḥ || 10. 9

སྐྱེས་པ་བུད་མེད་ལྷ་མོ་དང༌། །
བུད་མེད་ཀྱི་ནི་སྐྱེས་པ་ལྷ། །
རྡོ་རྗེ་པདྨ་སྦྱོར་བས། །
ཕན་ཚུན་དུ་ནི་མཆོད་པར་བྱ། །

Omniscient, omnipresent, all-pervading,
Free from all afflictions,
For him there is no disease, nor old age;
Death does not exist for him.
sarvajñaḥ sarvago vyāpī sarvakleśavivarjitaḥ |
na rogo na jarā tasya mṛtyus tasya na vidyate || 9. 10

ཀུན་ཤེས་ཀུན་འགྲོ་ཁྱབ་པ་པོ། །
ཉོན་མོངས་ཀུན་ལས་རྣམ་པར་འདས། །
དེ་ལ་ནད་དང་རྒས་པ་མེད། །
དེ་ལ་འཆི་བ་ཡོད་མིན་ཏེ། །

I am everyone, and I pervade everything,
Creating everything and destroying everything.
I possess all forms, I am the awakened one;
I am the creator, the destroyer, a powerful lord full of bliss.
sarvo 'haṃ sarvavyāpī ca sarvakṛt sarvanāśakaḥ |
sarvarūpadharo buddhaḥ kartā hartā prabhuḥ sukhī ||

བདག་ནི་ཀུན་ཏེ་ཀུན་ལ་ཁྱབ། །
ཀུན་བྱེད་ཀུན་གྱི་འཇིག་པ་པོ། །
ཀུན་གྱི་གཟུགས་འཛིན་སངས་རྒྱས་ཏེ། །
བྱེད་པོ་འཇོམས་པོ་བདག་བདེ། །

Artists

—Kalsang

Mark Kusek – markkusek1.myportfolio.com

Kalsang Phuntsok – Instagram link: <u>kalsi phun</u>

Margaret Michie – margeret.michie99@gmail.com

Anna Lieb-Dubino & B.Love – Tsakli Collection
https://www.vajraweb.org/

Cover Photo – *A rare, 18th century, two-tone gilt bronze figure of Vajradhara and Samantabhadri in union.*

Sacred Love
Buddhist Tantric Poems

© 2025 Sophia Dalle Rubenstein

ISBN: 978-0-9986278-9-2

Published by:
The Canelo Project
www.caneloproject.com

Book/Cover design: *Athena Steen*
Treasure Box below: *Kalsang Phuntsok*

https://www.instagram.com/dallesophia/?hl=en
https://www.facebook.com/sophia.dalle/

All proceeds go to the Tibetan Nuns Project

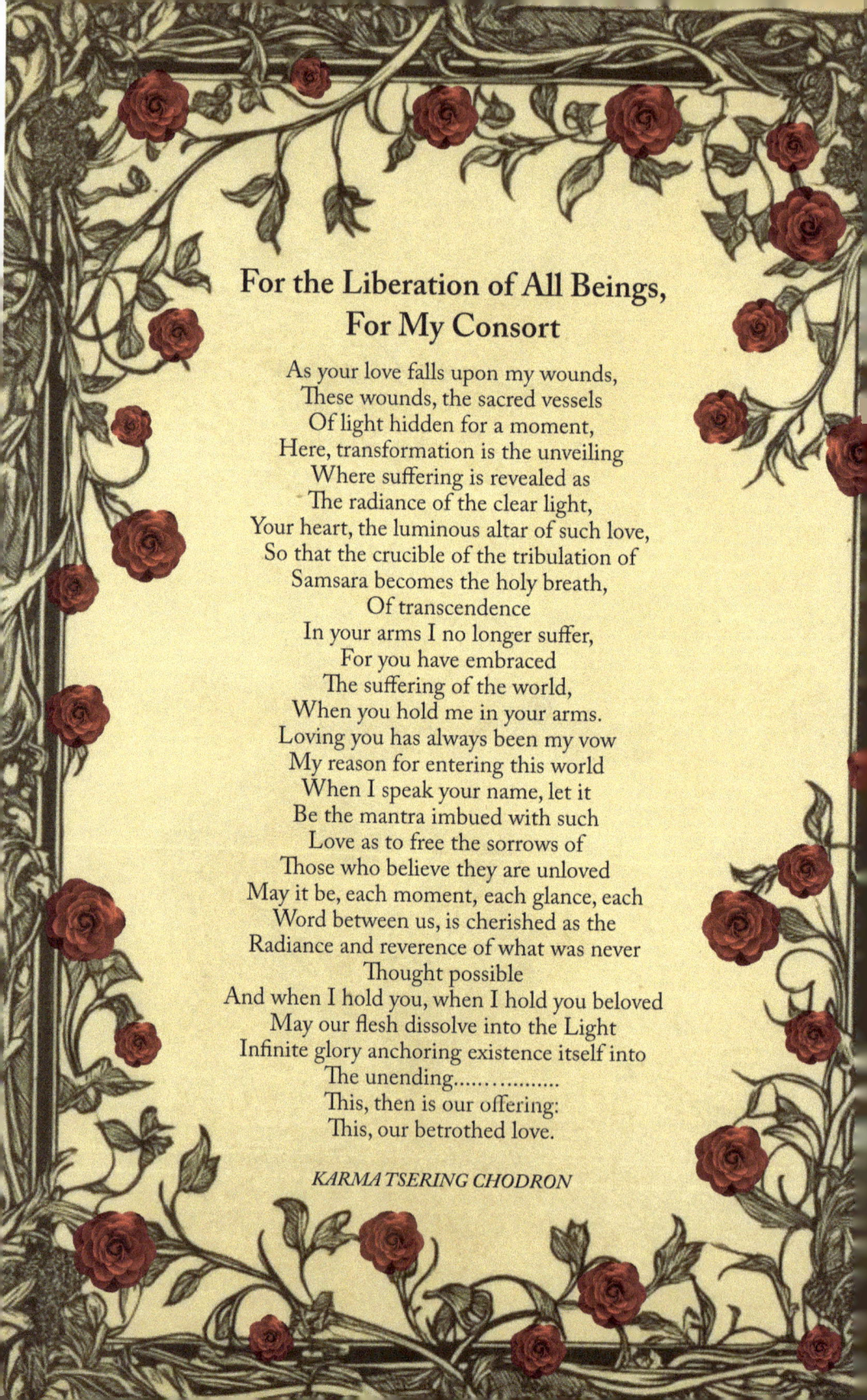

For the Liberation of All Beings, For My Consort

As your love falls upon my wounds,
These wounds, the sacred vessels
Of light hidden for a moment,
Here, transformation is the unveiling
Where suffering is revealed as
The radiance of the clear light,
Your heart, the luminous altar of such love,
So that the crucible of the tribulation of
Samsara becomes the holy breath,
Of transcendence
In your arms I no longer suffer,
For you have embraced
The suffering of the world,
When you hold me in your arms.
Loving you has always been my vow
My reason for entering this world
When I speak your name, let it
Be the mantra imbued with such
Love as to free the sorrows of
Those who believe they are unloved
May it be, each moment, each glance, each
Word between us, is cherished as the
Radiance and reverence of what was never
Thought possible
And when I hold you, when I hold you beloved
May our flesh dissolve into the Light
Infinite glory anchoring existence itself into
The unending……..……....
This, then is our offering:
This, our betrothed love.

KARMA TSERING CHODRON

www.ingramcontent.com/pod-product-compliance
Lightning Source LLC
Chambersburg PA
CBHW051058160426
43193CB00010B/1233